Natural Psychology

and

Human Transformation

(Revised)

by Na'im Akbar, Ph.D.

Foreword by Nathan McCall

Mind Productions & Associates, Inc.
324 N. Copeland Street
Tallahassee, FL 32304

Copyright 1995 by Na'im Akbar

All rights reserved. No part of this book may be reproduced in any form without written permission from the publishers, except by a reviewer who may quote brief passages in a review to be printed in a newspaper or magazine.

First Printing: January 1995
Second Printing: April 1996

Cover Design: Eugene Majied & Thomas Rasheed

Published by *Mind Productions & Associates, Inc.*
Tallahassee, Florida 32304

Library of Congress Catalog Card Number: 94-096278
ISBN 0-935257-04-7

Dedication

The Association of Black Psychologists
(Working to restore a Natural Psychology for all of humanity)

Acknowledgments

This project was made possible by the dedicated assistance of some very important people. The primary force behind the production of this book was the office staff at *Mind Productions*. This staff includes *Gloria Mu'min*, my executive secretary and mother-in-law; *Byron Thomas*, the orders manager; and *Rosalyn Nix*, the administrative assistant, who handled all of the word processing and constructed the complete layout for the text of this book. *Abdul Shakir* and *Diane Hall* edited the entire manuscript. *Nathan McCall* inspired the republication of this work by the laudatory comments he made about its earlier version in his remarkable novel, **Makes me Wanna Holler**. *Anwar Diop* and *Lester Bentley* encouraged me to pursue the project despite some early setbacks.

This book has been dedicated to the *Association of Black Psychologists* because of the important work this organization and its members have done for approximately twenty years in restoring a "natural" human psychology. A percentage from the sale of each of these books will be donated to the *Association of Black Psychologists* in order to further its work.

I am always grateful to my children, *Shaakira*, *Mutaqee* and *Tareeq*, who grant me time off from exercising my important duties as a father to engage in this work and all of my efforts of attempting to lift our people and salvage humanity in general.

There are always so many unnamed people who made a telephone call, dropped a note, or simply whispered a wish for my health and peace, never realizing how important they have been in keeping me strong in this daily struggle. As always, my thanks to *Allah* and our Ancestors.

FOREWORD

Several years ago while serving time in prison, I began the long and awkward struggle to understand the behaviors that had led me to such a tragic point. At that time, I knew I desperately needed to change my life which had been filled with crime, violence, and disregard for the lives of others. What I didn't know was how much change I was capable of bringing about.

During my incarceration, another inmate gave me a book that he said might shed some light on what I was attempting to accomplish. It was Na'im Akbar's **Natural Psychology and Human Transformation.**

I took the thin paperback to my cell and became fascinated by the author's description of the nature of human beings. In the book, Akbar asserted that we are more than the sum total of our actions and more than the makeup of our physical selves. He also indicated that the essence of us is spiritual and that, as creations of God, we have growth and development potential that reaches far beyond our limited--and limiting--perception of ourselves.

That assertion challenged my understanding of what I was. I had always thought of myself in tangible terms as a physical being. As a result, I had stumbled through life with little purpose beyond trying to satisfy my physical appetites.

After reading Na'im's book, it became apparent to me that my ability to lead a fulfilling and productive life had been severely restricted because my definition of myself had been so narrow. **Natural Psychology** *revealed to me a truth that was so simple that it had been so easy to overlook: That you can't reach your human potential if you don't know--fully--how much potential you have. In short, it gave me something higher for which to strive, something that I knew to which I was entitled, and could get if I applied myself.*

Shortly after being released from prison, I attended Norfolk State University and was surprised to learn that Na'im Akbar was a psychology professor there. I went to meet him and later enrolled in one of his courses. Needless to say, the ideas promoted in **Natural Psychology** *emerged as a recurring theme* *throughout the course, which remains the single most fulfilling formal educational experience I have ever had.*

Na'im and I eventually became good friends and remain so today. In the years since I first read his tome, I've often gone to my bookshelf and pulled out **Natural Psychology and Human Transformation** *to remind myself of the need to continue reaching for higher ground. With each new reading, I invariably discover some new insight or run across some timeless truism that I hadn't noticed before.* **Natural Psychology** *is just that kind of book--concise yet powerful, always relevant, and universal in its appeal. It's a handbook for life. Read it and grow.*

Nathan McCall
Author, **Makes me Wanna Holler**

TABLE OF CONTENTS

Introduction..i

From Grafted to Natural Psychology................................1

The Society and the Butterfly..21

INTRODUCTION

This small pamphlet was originally published in 1977. At that time I was directing the "Office of Human Development" for the (then) "World Community of Islam in the West," and serving as an aide to (then) Imam Wallace D. Muhammad. One of my responsibilities was to help prepare materials that would enhance the psychological development of the membership of the "World Community of Islam" as well as the broader community, based upon the teachings of (now) Imam Waarith Deen Mohammed. After 1979, when the organization of the World Community of Islam in the West was dissolved by Imam Mohammed, and I left this position, this book was taken out of print. In the course of the last fifteen years, numerous changes have come about in Imam Mohammed's organization, as well as his course and ideas.

I cannot determine what Imam Mohammed's thoughts might be on his ideas from that era now, but one of the important concepts which he emphasized at that point in his ministry was the importance of growth in the understanding of human development. As a psychologist, I seized upon this notion as a critical concept to develop because it seemed to be an important idea for us to understand ourselves better as human beings. I wrote the pamphlet as an extension of the Islamic ideas that Mr. Mohammed was at that time cultivating within the "World Community of Islam." Those Islamic teachings seemed very much compatible with the understanding of human beings that I was seeking as a correction to the clearly inadequate ideas of human functioning that I had acquired from my European-American, Judeo-Christian education in "psychology."

Growth and change are constants in nature. It is through the growth process (from the womb to the grave), that crude and primitive substance becomes refined and completed matter. The study of the mind of human beings in the Western World has suffered some very serious restrictions because of its limited concept of human growth. Western Psychology has reduced its concept of the mind of man to the limitation of man's physical body or his physical behavior. In doing so, *wo/man* has become entrapped in the limited arena of his/her physical body. *(This synthesis of woman and man is to underscore my clarity on the idea that "man" in the generic sense means women and men).* From the perspective of Western psychology, our thoughts, dreams and aspirations have become "biochemical processes in the brain" and our search for the truth of *the invisible* has been characterized as "hallucinatory experiences resulting from delusional distortions or behavioral dysfunctions based on conditioned avoidance responses." Our development has become restricted to our muscular maturation, changing perceptual skills, language acquisition, or the various expressions of our psychosexual energy. To the Western world, complete human development has become no more than the expansion of flesh, and man's human potential has been reduced to competition with the aging process.

With the loss of the proper concept of complete human growth, man's possibility for change has become seriously limited. Since change (according to Western theories) could only be affected through biochemical alterations or behavioral manipulations, we as human beings have become slaves to our own chemistry or our history of rewards and punishments. The dismal picture painted by Western Psychology is that man is locked into the limitations of his future learning capability. Such a picture has led to a great deal of pessimism about the possibilities for human change. The possibilities for human change are becoming more and more restricted as reflected in the rapid increase of mental illness, criminal and anti-social behavior, drug (including alcohol) abuse, and the many other indications of human waste and deterioration. The continued appeal to other chemical or behavioral solutions to these problems (with their poor success rate) shows the limitations of this *physical* conceptualization of human change.

My suggestion in this book is that the concepts of Western Psychology have produced an unnatural human being based upon its unnatural assumptions about human functioning and development. By converting the living inner being into a material being, man's potential to capture and master his animal form has been lost. In fact, the inner being (called *psyche* or *soul*) became a servant to the animal disposition identified by Western psychologists as the core of the human make-up. The

Introduction

loss of the real picture of the human being, which had grown in man's awareness of himself over centuries of study of his connection to the universe, has led to a retardation in the growth of the human life form.

From the earliest recorded time, men and women of inspiration and Divine guidance have brought a message of human growth and inspiration to the minds of people. These wise persons have helped to renew the failing species in its worst moments by bringing a message of hope which reminds us of our higher potential and of our transformational ability. This message reestablishes humanity's relationship with the natural order and reminds humanity that they are servants of a higher Truth and are equipped to develop themselves through the will that they have been given.

My plan had been to revise this book for several years, but so many other activities seemed to prevent its completion. This year, Nathan McCall published a highly successful autobiography called *Makes me Wanna Holler*. Nathan, who is a good friend of mine and a former student, mentioned *Natural Psychology and Human Transformation* as a handbook that had inspired him during a difficult and transitional period in his life. As a result of the extraordinary success of Nathan's work, tremendous interest was generated for this book, and the large volume of phone calls that came into my office requesting it served as the necessary impetus for me to revise the book and get it back into print.

Again, I must express my thanks to Imam W. D. Mohammed for the ideas which stimulated the initial writing of this book. I have chosen to apply the concepts to the specific needs of restoring the psychological functioning of African-American people. As is the case with all of my work, none of the concepts are limited to my particular cultural group, but my primary commitment is to heal and restore the historically oppressed and damaged African people. If these concepts did not have universal applicability then, they would be unusable as far as I am concerned. The fact that I choose to apply these universal concepts to the particular experience of my community is neither biased nor "racist" as some people have chosen to label such an African-centered approach. Being Afrocentric simply means that African people can understand the universe by beginning from the center of our experience and moving outward to encompass all of humanity. All knowledge should be relevant and relevance is established by the reference of a people's particular experiences. One of the serious psychological and intellectual problems of African people is that for the last 400 plus years we have tried to build a relevant reality looking at all ideas and at ourselves from the reference point of other peoples' particular experiences. We are seeking to rebuild our own reference point, not to oppress others, but to liberate ourselves.

Our hope is that this brief introduction to the concept of human transformation will have direct and immediate relevance to the healing of the historically oppressed people of African descent specifically, but will serve as a key to the upliftment of spiritually oppressed humanity in general. Perhaps the most significant aspect of the message of this book is that human beings have powerful, but untapped potential that has been obscured by false and erroneous messages about the true human nature. If we build on the images found in the natural world, we can rediscover the Truth of the essence of our real form. The message of Truth does not require advanced degrees, mastery of obscure religious concepts nor initiation in esoteric secret orders, but Truth can be taught by simply understanding the nature of a caterpillar and a butterfly. Read and prepare to fly!

Na'im Akbar, Ph.D.
Tallahassee, Florida
July 14, 1994

1.

FROM GRAFTED TO NATURAL PSYCHOLOGY

There are specific and predictable patterns in the created physical world. These patterns serve as an image for the structure of the natural world. The understanding of these patterns serves as the foundation for knowledge. Each human being rediscovers knowledge consistent with the way that mankind originally discovered knowledge, by observing and gradually understanding these patterns. Every mind enters the world in darkness with windows available through the senses which permit us to observe how nature is constructed. The infant enters the world flat on its back, arms and feet flailing in an uncoordinated fashion. Despite this initial darkness, this empty mind is soon able to begin its evolution towards genuine humanity. Having a living and functional mind is actually the criteria for membership in the human race. If you don't have a mind, you aren't alive yet. The infant learns to be a human being by interacting with the world around it.

Through this interaction, the infant learns that the created physical world has messages in it that actually serve the purpose of feeding the mental growth of the person. Knowledge begins in the real world and not in the heads of people. Certainly much of the knowledge that we acquire is transmitted from the minds of other people, but the foundation of knowledge is found imbedded in nature and her processes. This basic knowledge is called **"root knowledge"** because it serves as the foundation for all higher levels of knowing.

Root Knowledge and Grafted Knowledge

Probably the most basic message that's contained in this "root knowledge" is the idea of order, or a plan, in nature. The Ancients were able to formulate the basic principles of mathematics simply by observing themselves and the world around them. They were able to look at the heavens and observe alternating patterns of day and night, with the cadence being calculated by the phases of the moon. They were able to observe the change in seasons calculated by the location of the sun and the star formations. By observing their own bodies, they understood fundamental counting principles with ten being the foundation of the numbering system already illustrated by ten fingers and ten toes.

Another characteristic of the root knowledge is the idea that all things are interrelated. Ideas don't exist in separate and isolated disciplines or fields. Math is as connected with biology as it is connected with art, religion and economics. The fact that we sometimes focus only on one thing at a time is a consequence of our limited capacity for seeing and not a limitation in the way that reality is put together. So our theories of politics, philosophy or psychology represent a fragmented description of only a part of nature taken in isolation from the whole.

Probably the most basic idea that is acquired from the observation of nature is an appreciation for *order* and the presence of a *plan*. Anyone who has gone to bed at night with a sense of certainty that the sun would rise the next morning believes in a master plan. The person who looks out on a snow-covered field and confidently exclaims that "Spring is just around the corner," is not speaking to the knowledge of his senses, but he is responding to an understanding of the pattern or order in nature. Such minor observations are actually confirmation of belief in a basic and predictable plan. Without such a basic belief, every next minute is just a guess and a gamble. The obvious implication from the presence of such a precise plan is the recognition of a Planner.

Knowledge that is not based in this fundamental natural root knowledge is obviously unnatural. Such unnaturalness is what we mean when we refer to "grafted knowledge." A set of ideas which has taken what was natural and put them together with something that is either unreal or inappropriately combined, represents a deviant form of reality. Such a grafting misrepresents the natural order. An example of a grafted form of knowledge is one that presents an incomplete and distorted picture of nature's process and claims it to be the entire picture. If one observes that animals need food to survive and then concludes that food is the only thing that keeps animals alive, he is presenting grafted knowledge because of its incompleteness. Someone who concludes that a race horse is the fastest animal on earth without even bothering to look at the speed of an African cougar is presenting grafted knowledge. Though this fallacy is present in all fields of knowledge, it is most evident and most damaging as it relates to the knowledge regarding human functioning and development.

Our discussion is going to focus on how this grafting has created a very serious and distorted idea of the nature of the human being because of the grafted knowledge present in European-American psychology. We shall also point to some guidelines for reconstructing a "natural psychology" drawing upon indications from the natural world which will help us to distinguish the *real* from the *grafted*.

Grafted Psychology

Psychology represents an extremely important field of knowledge because it is the model for understanding the human being and the human potential. The images reflected in psychology serve as the basis for how people see themselves and their potential. In the ancient days, psychology did not exist as an objective science because the image of man was too large to fit into the narrow mode of objectivity. The human being was considered to be created in the image of God, therefore, his development and conduct were understood within the domain of theology rather than a science of psychology. Human beings were considered to follow the order of nature, but they were also capable of rising above the limitations of the physical or material world. So nature was used as a source for allegories or metaphors to describe the growth or evolution of man rather than a way to give direct images of man. Even though man's nature was considered to be orderly and controlled by the higher plan of a Planner, ordinary observation was considered inadequate for understanding man. The reason for this had much to do with man's ability to know but not to be known.

Human beings are born with fewer initial abilities than most animals. However, within a limited period of time, because of his learning capacity, man studies, imitates and quickly surpasses these animals who were his superior in size, speed, and instinct. Whereas other animals are obviously locked into the dictates of their particular nature (e.g. birds can fly and fish can swim), they cannot assume the nature of any other animal. The bird is a master of flying in the air, but those birds that are not water fowl cannot master swimming skills, because it is not in their nature. Human beings are born without the physical capacity to either swim or fly, but by observing the form of those animals that swim and fly, men construct ships and planes and, in short order, are able to out-perform those animals whose nature is to swim and fly. So human beings have had to look to higher and lower forms of nature in order to get an image of who they were and what they could potentially become.

Western psychology concluded that humans were subject to the same methods of observation or research as was the rat, dog, monkey or even the insect. With the rise of Western psychology, humans were demoted from their lofty status as a special form of life operating within nature. Such a demotion introduced the initial grafted knowledge of human development into world society. The exchange of the *literal* for the *metaphor* distorted our appreciation for what the processes of the natural world tell us about our human nature. This grafted form of psychology has several important characteristics which have rendered it inadequate in accounting for the full range of human creation and creativity. As we shall discuss later, we perhaps need to resort to other forms of knowledge rather than objective observation in order to understand the nature of a higher being who is *in* nature, but not *of* nature.

This European-American, Judeo-Christian based psychology which we accept as a universal description of human life is in fact quite limited in its grafted descriptions of the human nature. Even though there is diversity in the various "schools" or approaches to describing the human nature, they all carry one of several flaws which make the knowledge base grafted.

One of these qualities is the assumption that the essence of human life is its physical manifestation. This is an example of how the grafting process creates disastrous distortions. Undoubtedly, human beings occupy physical bodies which are subject to certain physical laws and are comparable to other physical forms in nature. The grafting process occurs when the total human nature is equated with its physical manifestation. This is the assumption in most of Western psychology. This physically based psychology essentially argues that "what you see is what you get." They argue that the human being can be reduced to his behavioral response to certain physical signs or stimuli. In fact, one very popular European school of psychology developed by William Sheldon concludes that we can predict the personality of people by identifying their body type, which literally suggests that human beings are a consequence of how their bodies look. The Freudian psychoanalytic types conclude that the human essence can be reduced to our physical needs or appetites. The Behavioral psychologists are the ones who conclude that there is nothing of any greater significance to humans than the way that they respond. It is important to remember that these conclusions are from root knowledge having its foundation in the observations of nature, but the grafting is the statement of these images as the total picture of the human being.

There is certainly no argument that a part of the human expression is what can be observed in our behavior. The grafting is the fragmentation of the total picture and the conclusion that these physical manifestations are the totality of the human nature. Despite considerable diversity in the ways that these European-American, Judeo-Christians discuss the human being, they all base their conclusions on certain physical expressions of the human life form.

Western psychology's conclusion that the outer observable nature of the human being is the best and most accurate picture of the human being has led to many of the faulty expressions so prevalent in European-American life. For example, people are thoroughly preoccupied with their material life as the essence of who they are. There is minimal attention given to the mental, moral or spiritual aspects of life in the Western world. In fact, the mental, moral and spiritual aspects gain their authenticity only as instruments of achieving certain material expressions. For example, the scholar is legitimized by his degrees rather than the examples of his accomplishments in improving human life. The successful wo/man is measured by their material wealth rather than their acquisition of peace, harmony and love. This image of the human being actually describes the objectives of human activity. There is precious little attention paid to the inner life of human beings in Western psychology. In fact, attention to the inner processes (even just as reflections of outer appetites such as the Freudian drives) are considered "poor science" since they give greater credibility to the inner nature rather than the outer form and its natural expression.

The other pervasive quality of Western psychology is its consistent representation of the superiority of Caucasian people. Its focus on the outer nature and the physical form permits them (Caucasian people) to equate their contemporary accomplishments in the material world with their human superiority. Not only do they make selections from history which place them in the most positive light (creating a *grafted* history), but they focus on those human qualities which suggest greater achievement for their particular human group. Much of the early history of American psychology, in particular, has sought to document the psychological, mental and intellectual superiority of Caucasian people over people of color. (The reader is directed to the outstanding documentation of this idea in the books by Alexander Thomas and Samuel Sillen entitled *Racism and Psychiatry* and Robert Guthrie's *Even the Rat Was White*). This quality of white supremacy pervades Western psychology despite the particular school of psychology to which they may ascribe. From the pscholanalysts to the psychometricians, the conclusion is that the best way to be human is to be a Caucasian, Judeo-Christian male of European descent.

White supremacy is another example of how the grafting process influences the knowledge base. The fact that the knowledge of Western psychology is primarily based on the observations of European-American Caucasian males observing people just like themselves provides the foundation of accurate observations inappropriately attributed to an entire population. Their failure to incorporate the observations made by and of other people of Earth makes their conclusions not only inaccurate in terms of *what* they observe but also inaccurate from the limitations of *who* they observe.

Natural Psychology

Natural psychology should emerge from observations of human life in the natural world, but it must be evaluated consistent with the patterns of nature. It must take into account the full variety of the human experience as a criteria for assessment of the true nature of human beings. Nature will offer images of what the human potential is about and those images must be understood as symbols or indicators of what the non-observable inner human potential is about.

In the essay that follows, we discuss one of nature's most compelling images of transformation. This image of the transformation of the butterfly is presented as an allegory for the same kind of invisible transformation that takes place within the mental and spiritual development of the human being. We suggest that although human beings are not literally like caterpillars and butterflies, this natural image reveals some important ideas about the developing and evolving human life. For the purposes of our discussion, we are emphasizing this type of image from nature as the kind of concept which must be incorporated into a "natural psychology." This concept of transformation is suggested as a critical one to fully appreciate the vastness of the human potential and the human nature. Even though transformation is implied in most of the grafted conceptions of human psychology, its full implication as a description of human **spiritual** growth is not considered. This idea is usually discussed as "developmental" psychology, but the emphasis is on the physical growth as an indication of the potential for human growth. If it is not physically based as Freud's oral, anal and phallic stages, then it is behaviorally based like Piaget or some of the other cognitive (i.e., thought) developmental psychologists.

There are a couple of assumptions which we must entertain in order to understand the concepts of "natural" psychology as opposed to Western "scientific" psychology. One of these assumptions is that human beings are fundamentally spiritual entities whose physical forms are only reflections or a material expression of their true spiritual nature. With this assumption, we understand that the physical form is always an incomplete picture of what the human being is all about. So the limitations of ideas which guide our thought about material reality do not apply to spiritual reality. For example, physical things fit within the narrow confines of time and space. They can be understood as simple "cause and effect" relationships and can be validated by one or more of the five senses. Spiritual "substance" is timeless, not confined to any single space, and its true nature can only be inferred from the physical manifestations. Since this is the nature of spiritual reality then, the second assumption suggests that we can understand the spirit through another set of skills other than those used by scientific investigation.

There are ways of "knowing" other than through the observational skill used in the scientific method. One of these other observational methods is "intuition," where there is an emotional cue based on some unobservable indication which comes to us through the unconscious. This is the well-known phenomenon of the "hunch" that tells you that something good or bad is about to happen or the "vibe" that this is a good person or a bad person with whom you can socialize. These are not "objective" ways of knowing, but they guide much of what we understand about the world and especially about people. In parts of the world that have not been consumed by reliance on the physical and the senses as its total source of information, "intuition" is accepted as a more valuable tool for "knowing" than "observing."

The other method of observation to which we must turn in seeking to understand this spiritual nature of human beings is yet another method that has no credibility in the grafted psychology. This method is "revelation," which is of course a word of blasphemy in the scientific world of Western psychology. To them, revelation is relegated to folklore and religion but it has no credibility in terms of so-called "objective" reality.

Most other cultures and people other than European-Americans have always given preeminent credibility to revelation. In the Western world, such insights are described as superstitious at best and more likely considered in the same vein as the hallucinations of psychotics. Of course, the Western Judeo-Christian tradition accepts revelation within the confines of their religious beliefs, but the conflict between science and religion in the West is a conflict rooted in the higher credibility given to material reality and the general suspiciousness of spiritual concepts. Even worse is the tendency on the part of Western religious people to interpret and validate their spiritual notions using material criteria (e.g., the search for Noah's ark or the shroud of Jesus). They use the material criteria instead of appreciating the superior meaning of these ideas as spiritual concepts rather than ones that can gain validation by applying the materially-based "scientific" method.

With a proper spiritual understanding, there is much important information contained in the ancient Kemetic *Book of Coming Forth by Day* (commonly referred to as the *Egyptian Book of the Dead*.) The *Holy Bible*, the *Torah* and the *Holy Qur'an* all contain significant and important insights from revelation. They must be understood utilizing spiritual criteria and not material criteria, however. One quality of understanding revelation is knowing that you cannot understand the "language of revelation" in any literal way. Language can only point to the true spiritual reality which eludes language and observation. We must understand analogy, metaphor and symbolism as a means of fully appreciating what the books reveal. We must also approach the books of revelation with the kind of open-mindedness shared by those who received the revelations. Of course, the many religious wars which the world has endured are a consequence of the claims of various interpreters that they have a superior understanding for the messages in these books.

The Sufis (or mystics of Islam), which are the source of one set of interpretations, have brought important understanding to a concept of human transformation that is revealed in the *Holy Qur'an*. The Sufis, like many Christian mystics, have sought to understand the spiritual meaning and interpretation of the books of revelation. They are unlike many of the "non-

Natural Psychology and Human Transformation

mystical" scholars who have tended to apply material criteria in trying to understanding these revealed books. (Reflect on how we perceive even the image of a "mystic" as a strange, otherworldly and clearly non-reliable source of information). Jews, Christians and Muslims all claim that their books reflect, in whole or part, revelation which has come through the spiritual insights of those who were most developed in their religious tradition or closest to (The) God. As an example of how natural psychology conceptualizes the human transformation process, I am going to draw upon the interpretations given to the stages of human growth found within the revelation of Prophet Muhammad (PBUH) which is the *Holy Qur'an*.

Stages in the Transformation Process

The first of these stages is referred to as the *nafs all*a *ammarah* (in Qur'anic Arabic) or the "hungering self or soul." This initial stage of being is characterized by the force of hunger as the essential orientation of the self. This hungering self is the quality to which most of the Western psychologists limit their understanding of the human being. Freud's "Id," which is his concept of the essence of the personality, is certainly best described as the "hungering self." Freud postulates that the Id continues to be the primary force of the personality always seeking to control and maintain dominance over the total personality. This initial stage of growth is concerned about satisfying needs, maintaining comfort, and forging the rudiments of physical survival. This disposition dictated by the need to survive in the physical world lays the foundation for our connection with the material world and is characterized by its preoccupation with the needs of the body. It is this basic and most fundamental part of the human make-up which has perhaps served to validate the focus of the Western psychologists on the material components of the self.

Certainly, this drive of desire or hunger forces the person to reach out into the material world around him. In fact, this hunger serves as the natural foundation for a component of the self which must endure throughout the life of the self. The desire must evolve to a higher stage of expression, otherwise you are left with a *physical* being rather than a *human* being. What begins as physical desire soon becomes curiosity and curiosity transforms to ambition; ambition into aspiration, and ultimately, aspiration into transcendence. This is the same hunger that initially drives the person to feed her body but it is experienced differently as it transforms and evolves.

The second stage of transformation based upon the *Holy Qur'an*, is the "self-accusing soul" called *nafs al lawamah* in Arabic. The self-accusing or rational man is not one driven by desire, but he actively intervenes in his own experiences. Whereas the hungering man can be manipulated by conditioning (the tool of choice of the behavioral psychologists), the self-accusing man is above the passive posture required for effective behavior modification. Only when the mentality of the person is arrested or untransformed to a higher self-accusing self can that person be effectively controlled by behavior modification. Of course, one can be arrested in their development by being put into a retarding environment (like most of America's prisons or other institutions which are unnatural in their influence on human development) and stimulate deformation rather than transformation.

The self-accusing self, as this translation of the Arabic implies, involves the ability to "accuse" or "critique" oneself. This speaks to the simultaneous emergence of one's rational capacity for reflection and evaluation, but simultaneously enhances the person's ability for critical self-evaluation or accusation. Reasonable conduct and moral conduct are not contradictory in this concept as it tends to be in the rational *versus* emotional dichotomy that one finds within grafted notions of psychology. So this stage of the self's transformation stands above the self of hunger. As we described above, the hungering self drives the person based upon desire. The "self-accusing" soul is more self-determining and is capable of exercising influence over the appetites. Under the influence of this stage of the self's evolution, hunger becomes curiosity and ambition rather than the blind passion of desire. The self-accusing stage is characterized by *conscience* (the evaluative or moral voice in the soul), as well as *consciousness*, which is the rational or knowledgeable part of the soul.

The person in the stage of *nafs al lawamah* is no longer subject to the influences of the environment and can no longer be understood as just a responsive and behaving entity. But he or she has become a determining and independent agent within the physical environment. In order for this knowing soul to develop, she must obtain true and living knowledge which guides the continued and proper growth and development of the soul. The knowledge that is required at this stage is not just the knowledge of the senses but it must be the higher knowledge of Truth. It is the kind of knowledge that the Ancients referred to as "Divine utterance." It is the Divine guidance that comes from religious or spiritual Truth which provides an interpretation of the experiences from the environment. It is the kind of metaphysical knowledge that provides both a rational and moral understanding of reality. This kind of knowledge improves the person's capacity as a "self-accusing soul." Being self-accusative does not mean that one is consumed with a guilty conscience or preoccupied with their faults. Instead, it means that one is able to interpret her experiences within the elevated context of seeing oneself in pursuit of higher goals.

Grafted knowledge retards the person's ability to be transformed into this higher state of being. For example, false knowledge influences people to believe that they are limited to their physical selves and controlled by their physical appetites. They believe that their physiques or figures determine their worth as people. False knowledge equates "knowing" with the amount of material that is memorized rather than the material that is actually understood. Annual income is equated with success in life. One's address, social connections or the car that one drives is the criteria by which people evaluate their worth and their advancement. False knowledge actually arrests human development by creating false or phony people. For example, in Western psychology the experts in child development are frequently people who either have no experience in rearing their own children or have done a remarkably poor job in doing so. The second highest rate of professional suicides is among psychiatrists who are supposedly the "experts" on the human mind. This shows that even though they are certified by the American Psychiatric Association, they are not certified by the *True* knowledge of human life. One would expect that those who claim such expertise would be in much greater mastery of their own lives. A society that evaluates success by mastery of materially based knowledge can only create people with a limited understanding of reality. The importance of this message of transformation is to help us to appreciate the higher criteria for human growth. Not only does it require us to be more self-accusative in evaluating our own advancement, but it better equips us to understand the people around us and their level of advancement relative to the ultimate human destiny.

Ironically, many of those who claim to be the experts in religious knowledge are poor examples of having mastered the higher spiritual notions which they espouse. The scandals surrounding the televangelists in recent years is a good indication of how improperly understood and applied religious ideas do not necessarily feed the higher spiritual appetites that actually transform the person and feed their continued growth. This does not mean that people who have arrived at *nafs al lawamah* are flawless and perfect. We know that the struggle with the hungering self is a lifetime struggle. The presence of struggle does not indicate failure to advance. The self-accusative soul helps us to gain increasing mastery over the lower appetites and gives us more control over the forces which oppose our growth. It also helps us to understand that self-mastery is an asset of our personal growth and is not done in response to a punitive Divine being who sits waiting to "zap" us for violation of Divine laws. The consciousness of this stage of growth lets us know that Divine law is the path of growth and we "zap" ourselves by our failure to gain control over our lower self. The consciousness of this stage makes us want to grow and transform desire into the kind of ambition and aspiration which stimulates our appetite for Truth, understanding and self-mastery. This is the difference between real and false people. The false people have no actual aspiration for growth, which is indicative of the fact that they are still under the influence of the gravity of the hungering self which arrests them in their development as completed human beings.

The final stage of the self to come into birth is the *nafs al mutma'innah*. This is the completed self, the self that has found rest. After gaining the capacity for self-accusation and acquiring the appetite for Truth and growth, the soul proceeds towards its evolved state as a "butterfly," which we will describe in another section of this book. This soul which has come to rest relates naturally to higher meanings of the symbols of nature. Such a person sees the natural environment in its fullness. This person appreciates that "nature" feeds the body, the mind and the soul--a proper "diet" on the ingredients from which the natural world produces fully healthy people. With this kind of understanding the developing person is able to incorporate into the self from nature, the messages of transformation, harmony, righteousness and peace.

The soul that is at rest also comes to understand the death process. It comes to know that the soul does not die, but like all energy, it just transforms. The tree ceases to live, but it doesn't die. It becomes a part of a new life process called "rot" which actually feeds the very life that it produced in its earlier life process. Our physical bodies will similarly cease to live, but will actually only be transformed back into the elements of their origin. The body will become the sacrificial lamb to this creation which gave it its birth. The potassium of the individual physical body will reunite with the potassium of the "Mother Earth" which gave it birth. The carbon will re-join the carbon. The gases that fill our bodies will reunite with the community of gases from which they came. The waters that constitute the vast majority of our bodies return to the waters of life out of which all life emerged. Physical attributes are no more than forms which actually constitute a language which the soul at rest learns to read. The "souls at rest" become the wise men and women of our communities who set the traditions and understand the higher Truths.

In the same way that the physical elements came to life and formed the body, the mental elements came together and gave birth to a mind. The thing that feeds that mind is the Truth that is embedded in the creation. So long as the creation lives, the mind that it creates will live. As our consciousness of the "whole" creation expands, we grow to a greater awareness of the Creator. The perfect (or Holy) form of the Creator lets us know our potential through submission to the Truth that makes up his form. The ultimate concept of death, which is simply another picture of transformation, lets us understand that what is physical will re-join the physical; what is mental will stand with the mental images of creation, and what is Divine will stand with the Divine form reuniting the dispersed spiritual energy with its spiritual source.

The soul that is at rest is able to read the messages of creation on all levels. This person is able to see a tree, eat the fruit from the tree and at the same time see in the tree an image of the form of the man. The man must root himself in physical reality like the tree roots itself in the earth, and reach for the higher reality as the tree reaches for the sun. When the wo/man grows up to the light of the higher world, he spreads forth foliage which is supplied by food from below and light from above. The freed soul at rest sees a mighty ocean, but also sees the moral capacity of the human life. Moral life (like water), which always reaches its own level, is capable of cleansing all kinds of dirt and is a force that is actually capable of transforming the earth (the physical form). This is no doubt the origin of the ritual of baptism in Christianity and Wudu (the ritual washing done by Muslims prior to prayer) in Islam. The water is intended to symbolize the cleansing or transforming of the earth--body--in order to free the spirit or experience the spiritual nature.

The ability to read these multiple levels of meaning gave rise to the ancient African wise men who determined that all matter is composed of the four elements of earth, fire, air and water. These wise persons had come into a knowledge, not only of the simplicity of life in its essential form, but also an appreciation for the multiple levels of meaning found metaphorically in the basic elements of creation. These elements of the material world also have symbolic meaning to the mental and spiritual world which can be readily understood by the soul that has come to rest. The rest does not mean that all activities cease, the rest is in reference to the return to oneness with the creation and Creative force that brought us into existence. To come to oneness with this force is the achievement of peace by Submission to the Divine oneness. The rest is also freedom from the struggle of the lower "nafs," since this soul has fully submitted itself to identification with the God-force within itself.

The completed soul understands that it is formed by the creation, formed by Divine revelation and that it must form itself. We make ourselves by the decisions and choices that we make about our lives. When we submit ourselves to weakness or to materialism, we grow into a weak materialistic form. When we give ourselves to negativism, anger or sadness, we grow into those forms. When we give ourselves to fear, then we become fearful. The fact is that we take on the form to which we submit our consciousness. If we submit our consciousness to weakness or to lowly things, then the nature of our human make up will take on that form. In the same sense, if we submit ourselves to higher things like (The) God, Truth, spiritual goals, happiness, peace, love, etc., then we grow into those forms.

This is what human freedom is all about: We are influenced by the creation and the events of the physical world, but we are not subject to those influences, because our capacity for choice permits us to rise above their influence. Even our own emotions and inner feelings can influence us, but they do not control us because we have the capacity to rise above those influences through the power of will. We were made free of the rule of instinct so that we could become rulers of the earth (which includes our own bodies). This can only be done through submission to the higher principles in life, i.e., belief in the Truth of *The One God* (known as *Allah, Jehovah, Ja, Yahweh, Amen Ra, Onyame, Obatala*, and by many other names). Through submission to this higher force, we grow in that form. Then we must exercise our will through self-discipline and self-mastery and rise above the gravity of our lower form that is pulled by appetites and the conflicts of reason. We must first become rulers within ourselves so that we can grow consistent with our highest possibilities.

Perhaps, we can understand one of the images which we find in the Gospels which sheds light on the hungering self, the self-accusing soul, and the soul at rest. The Gospel image of the Trinity can perhaps be understood as the same transformational process personified in the form of the Father, the Son and the Holy Ghost. (Remember above, we have suggested that revelation is a spiritual language and not a literal one. So, we are not arguing for proof or disproof empirically, rationally or emotionally that there is a literal Trinity). We are suggesting a possible spiritual interpretation of a symbolic image which otherwise has no rational or empirical proof. Perhaps the Father represents the earth or the physical self; the first level of being manifested in the hungering or materially guided self. The Son could represent the rational mind of the self-accusing spirit. The Holy Ghost would represent the soul at rest which gives us wings--not literal angelic wings--but wings on the soul as depicted by the ancient Africans of Kemet (Egypt), which showed the Ba as a bird with a human head and arms. This Holy Ghost gives us wings to fly over the chaos and struggle of confusion and go directly to the Truth which places us immediately into heaven. Inspired by such a development, the soul is able to walk with **The God** while also walking with the fool on Earth. One is able to be on the asphalt of this world's roads while being on the streets paved with gold in the higher world. Once real knowledge has become your knowledge and once the power of Truth has become your power and once you have become a ruler within yourself, then you are in heaven right away.

Conclusion

Natural psychology is intended to give us a true picture of our nature and real potential as fully evolved human beings. The point of this discussion has simply been that grafted psychology gives a distorted and retarded image of the human being and our human capabilities. So long as we see ourselves only partially and imperfectly, then we can never become who we really are and we continue to replicate the false images which the false notions of psychology perpetuate. The character of people who find themselves in the Western world or under its influence has been deteriorating at an increasing rate. This human deterioration is not, as some would argue, the consequence of the declining influence of the "church." Instead, I would argue that this human deformation is a consequence of being increasingly under the influence of grafted notions of the human being. The more that the culture understands itself as being sexually driven, aggressively subjugated and materially determined, then that culture produces sexually preoccupied, aggressively-driven and materialistic people. This limited image of human beings has produced a culture of very limited people.

We can grow as human beings once again only when we obtain an exalted vision of our human capability. Some people find such an exalted image in religion. Increasingly people are looking to the motivational experts who speak to the higher human possibility, but only as a mechanism to achieve material and economic success. We must restore a natural and powerful psychology of human beings which will help the human family regain its vision of its true potential. These examples of the developing *nafs* or self taken from the Islamic tradition, do not suggest that Muslims are any more adept in developing this vision than any other religious people. In fact, we are finding that as Muslims around the world come more under the influence of the grafted images of the Western world, they are developing the same character flaws and arrested development that is so common in the Judeo-Christian world. As people lose contact with the natural psychology, they are subject to the loss of their higher image of their own possibilities. Consequently, there is a deterioration in their human character.

The crusade must be one that will restore the higher human vision. We must work to reestablish a view of ourselves which will put us back on the spiritual path of growth and in the company of the Most High. The work of the Afrocentric scholars, though greatly criticized as racist, ethnocentric and secular, is actually in the vanguard for the restoration of such thought. This scholarship has penetrated the Black church and has restored its transforming influence on the people who have embraced this vision, not of Black or African superiority, but of human excellence. This image, which has been the mainstay of many Black nationalist movements, has always had a powerfully transforming influence on those persons who began to see themselves in this exalted light. The great success of the Honorable Elijah Muhammad, Marcus Garvey and others is a consequence of the resurgence of the exalted human vision that their adherents accepted. Though the focus of the Afrocentric scholars is on the restitution of the historically oppressed people of African descent, the vision which is being developed is one, the only one, that will save all of humanity. That message essentially says, "We are of Divine origin manifested in material form with a path of gradual transformation guided by self-knowledge and self-mastery which will eventually restore us to a state of peace and spiritual consciousness in the form of our Creator." This is our natural potential and it must be the image cultivated by a *natural psychology*. Once this state of higher evolution is achieved, then like the butterfly, we will fly in the heavens of Truth, righteousness, harmony and peace. It is not our role to exclude anyone from this vision. It is our role to affirm this vision for ourselves and for our people who have been given a faulty and alien dream intended to degrade and enslave them rather than a vision of their true human greatness and possibility.

2.

THE SOCIETY AND THE BUTTERFLY

Traditional Teachers of Wisdom as well as the Divine scriptures of Revelation have always pointed to nature as the language of the Divine Mind. The people of ancient Kemet (called Egypt) actually referred to this language of the Divine as the *(ntrs) Neters* from which the word "nature" is derived. The guidance of these ancient Teachers suggests that if we look at the processes of the rising and setting sun, the growth and life cycles of trees and flowers, the lives of insects and other animals, we can find Divine direction for human lives. What is built into the natural processes of life are actually instructions for how man can more effectively develop himself consistent with the Divine format for his existence.

There is in the study of nature, a statement about growth, development, life and death of man. The unique quality of wo/man is that he must discover, with his consciousness, the path which his development must take. In this process, s/he is actually the handicapped being of creation, in that he does not automatically know and follow his nature. The human being, though, is also the master of nature in that s/he can discover and select to perfect his nature consistent with the creative power of the Divine. Nature contains so many keys to the understanding of our proper functioning, growth and yes, even our downfall, therefore, we are compelled to understand something about the world in which we live. This world in which we live is a book of pictures laid out for those who may never learn the meaning of words. It is a book that is opened wide for those who do not have an extensive vocabulary. In fact, even the infant, through its senses, can almost immediately begin to read and internalize this book of the natural world. Humanity's very first Divine book is the book of *Nature*.

This Divine Book must be approached with respect and humility, however. Nature cannot be approached with a desire to abuse or exploit. Neither can we approach nature with an attitude of idolatry, thinking that the processes revealed in her is in fact Divinity itself. We look to nature because, as a tool of the Divine, she points to the path of Truth (called *Ma'at* by the ancient Kemetic people). Nature is a part of the creation which emanates from the Creator. Through revelation and the tradition of our human ancestors, there is evidence that much of man's social, technical and spiritual development has been modeled on the images of nature. We are taught that if we study what nature does, we can get a message about what humans should be doing in order to keep their nature properly aligned with the natural processes.

In this discussion, we want to look at only one of those highly instructive processes in nature. It is a process that we find throughout nature with a consistent occurrence which makes it clear that it must be an essential part of the map for understanding the realities of human existence. This process is the one of *transformation*. It has clear applicability to human and societal growth, it is probably most vividly portrayed in the natural image of the butterfly.

A butterfly lays an egg. It is a fertilized egg. Within the confines of the egg is the male and female butterflies' contribution to the future life form. In fact, the egg contains, in a coded form, the entire ancestral contribution to this new life. All of the contributions from thousands of years of evolution are contained in this microscopic egg. At this point the egg is not actually life, but it is potential life. It is an unborn life, but a fertile and gifted life. The path which takes this potential life to actual life is the process of growth or transformation. The key to the realization of the hidden potential found in the microscopic egg is its destiny to unfold through the equally divine mechanism of growth. In fact, it is the very nature of this life process to grow, but it must have the proper growth environment in order to realize its potential.

After a few weeks and under the right conditions, the egg begins to open. Careful observation reveals that it doesn't really open, but it rather dissolves or disintegrates into another form. For a brief period of its disintegration, it is of a rather nondescript form, changing rapidly as occurs with all the decay processes in what appears to be death. In any event, in rather short order, this bubbly dissolving formless blob becomes a worm-looking creature with well-defined structures and mobility.

This new creature is what we affectionately refer to as a "hairy worm." The curiosity continues, though, because this egg that was laid by a beautiful adult butterfly comes into life, not in the appearance of its lovely, colorful, celestial parent, but as a creepy, crawly, slimy, hairy worm--a caterpillar. This newly developed creature bears absolutely no resemblance to the parent of its origin. There is certainly no evidence that this creature has any of the gifts which, we have argued, lay hidden in the codes of the egg which initiated its life form. It, in no way, resembles a butterfly. Even the worm's own mother would look at it in disbelief and declare: "Oh, no! This cannot be my child, because it bears no resemblance to me." But, as we shall see, such a mother would be one with limited vision to disown her yet unfamiliar offspring on such a superficial basis. In fact, such a mother would have had to have lost sight of her own history in order to make such a claim.

The "Hairy" Worm

So what accounts for the move from the storage house of the egg to becoming the distasteful looking hairy worm? The worm has a story to tell as does every other component of nature. The worm has an important function and an important tale to tell about our development as human beings as well. The worm has a very crucial function for the life of the insect. It establishes the foundation for the survival of this life form. The caterpillar has one essential function, and that is to feed. Its function is exclusively that of a physical entity. It has no celestial function; it has no physical beauty to show; it has no social and reproductive function. It is selfish, greedy and all consumed by its physical function of feeding itself.

This worm is consumed by consumption. It wants to eat all of the time. In fact, it doesn't even sleep but eats throughout the night and day. The caterpillar crawls among the leaves, and eats, eats, eats. In fact, with a few caterpillars present, an entire tree can actually be stripped of its leaves in a matter of days. They eat large multiples of their body weight in the course of a day. The major concern of the worm is feeding the physical being. His business is exclusively physical business. His very form and his natural orientation is to effectively take care of the job of the physical and material needs of the entity which is coming forth.

As a result of so much eating, the little hairy worm begins to grow rapidly. In a few days, it sheds one layer of skin and another layer of skin, larger and more developed, emerges. It isn't long before it is a big, fat, hairy worm. Though its unsightly form continues, the worm is growing and developing- consistent with its nature.

Interestingly enough, even with its amazing appetite and capacity for consumption, the caterpillar does not eat indiscriminately. Its instinct (or nature) directs it to the proper leaves with the proper nutrition to feed its growth in the most appropriate way. His choices are clocked into its nature consistent with the best instruction of his ancestral worms. Guided by the Divine nature of its own growth, instinctively it stays away from those things which are not conducive to its growth and survival. The Divine nature of his being propels him towards those things that are necessary for his proper growth and effective development. Because he consumes well and correctly, he expands materially and becomes very successful as a physical being.

The Cocoon

After a while, the worm achieves satisfaction and reaches a new level of maturity. After reaching physical maturity, he begins to regurgitate a substance from his mouth which forms a fine and elegant fiber. He begins (in accord with the pattern laid down in his nature) to wrap himself into his spittle (the fiber which comes from his mouth). He rolls himself into this new covering known as a cocoon. After a period of time, he completely encloses himself in this small pouch. With the submergence of himself into the cocoon, the entity takes on an entirely different appearance. The hairy worm is no longer to be seen. The voracious and mobile eater is gone and another inanimate form appears wrapped like an ancient mummy. It shows every indication of being lifeless with neither mobility nor observable life activity. For the second time in the life process of this entity, we see an amazing resemblance to what we call "death." As we noted in the case of the ostensible "death" process of disintegration of the egg, it only hastened the emergence of the new level of being in the form of the caterpillar.

So what is there to be learned from the cocoon. It is another stage in the life process with some distinct features just as we found in the caterpillar. In the first place, the quality of the cocoon depends greatly on the nourishment obtained through the eating of the worm. If the worm fails to obtain the right kind of leaves, then he won't be able to produce the fine quality fiber which will insure a well-formed cocoon. The biologists tell us that if the leaves do not have adequate moisture, the cocoon will actually disintegrate and the development process will be terminated. Leaves which have not received adequate sun to develop proper nutrition will keep the worm alive, but will not be effective in supplying the high quality fiber that is necessary to form a proper cocoon. A proper cocoon must be able to protect and support the developing life as it goes through the necessary process of transformation.

The cocoon is a vital shield for the continued development of the life form. It offers the necessary environment to feed proper growth for the continued evolution of this potential life form, which still has not reached its true potential as destined by the code of its genesis. The character of this cocoon strongly depends on what was consumed during the physical stage. Though apparently guided by greed and appetite in the worm stage, its very conduct determines the future life which follows it. The caterpillar submits appropriately to its nature. It also naturally relinquishes its form for a higher form when that time has come. Perhaps we can imagine an abnormal caterpillar that keeps on eating when sleeping time has come, but we cannot imagine such a caterpillar existing in a natural environment. Perhaps, in a contaminated or diseased environment, such a breakdown in nature might occur, but the nature of the butterfly has already dictated the course of its development.

We can more clearly see the great task of the human being who must make selections to grow itself properly. Unlike all other components of nature, the human being's capacity for abnormality is greater than all other forms of life. Its capacity for greatness is also greater than all other forms of life if it makes the proper choices consistent with its best possibilities. Man does not automatically know that he has a capacity to be something greater than his most basic form. Man can so easily become a permanent worm or disintegrate into a formless blob unrecognizable to even his own kind. He must make choices and be taught the full capability that the Creator has given to him.

The Birth of the Butterfly

Within the cocoon, another miracle begins to occur. "Death begins to shed its illusion and a new life begins to form." The life that had existed as a worm is no longer the predominant life of this entity. The worm has "died" in the cocoon and its transformation to a higher form of life has begun. Only vestiges of the old hairy worm-life remain present. Even its earthly mobility and multiple legs have been paralyzed and the life of the caterpillar as we knew it is no more. But his life during transformation is fed with the nourishment which he consumed in his worm-life. Life can be maintained within the cocoon sometimes only for weeks and sometimes through multiple seasons. But enough nourishment has been retained to protect life in the course of the womb. So, not only has the voracious eating and persistent work in the worm-life supplied the substance to encircle and secure the developing new life, but it has also preserved the substance to feed the life yet to come.

In due time, a new life form emerges from the cocoon. Alas, it is the butterfly in the form of its original parent; a big,

The Society and the Butterfly

beautiful, colorful butterfly. This butterfly which started as an egg and became a worm, went into a cocoon and emerged from the cocoon as a newly developed life form that doesn't have to crawl anymore. It doesn't have to eat leaves anymore because it is able to fly and can eat from the skies through which it glides. It drinks of the nectar from the flowers and moves to the awe and envy of all who would seek to make it their prey. It is no longer vulnerable to the feet of the society as was its precedent form--the caterpillar. The only reminder of the vulnerable worm is the body torso which is retained and now lifted aloft by the flamboyant wings which rise above the trees and above the heads of the beasts who so recently would have taken its life in the vulnerable form of the earthly traveler.

The new and lovely butterfly no longer repels human sensitivities as did the hairy worm which previously represented this life form. These same humans who were so recently repelled by his very appearance take personal risks just to observe him. The threat to his existence comes more from a desire to capture and retain him rather than to destroy and eliminate him. Even his recently repelled enemy wants to immortalize his beauty and display it as a relic of nature's great artistry. How ironic that one of the most repulsive sights (a slimy, hairy worm) has become one of the most coveted ones, the beautiful, colorful, delicate beauty of the butterfly.

This metamorphosis has radically changed the expression of this same life form. The life is the same, though its expression has changed radically. What had begun as just a blob of "potential" in the expression of larva or egg has at last become what it was intended to be: a reflection of the beautiful life which first spawned its existence. Though the life has remained the same, its expression has persistently and systematically transformed until it has come to resemble the life that originally gave it its being. Probably if this worm could talk, it would have proclaimed in despair the apparent hopelessness of its plight. It would, no doubt, have cried out in despair: "Oh, God, why me? Why must I be a worm, vulnerable and repulsive to human sensitivities?" Certainly if the worm had consciousness, but no vision of its ultimate possibilities, it would have bemoaned its pitiable condition.

But, as we know, the caterpillar proceeds secure in its instinct to simply do its best within the confines of its natural dispositions. He is programmed to respond without complaint to the full domain of his plight. The karmic redemption is in his ultimate salvation as the reborn incarnation of the beauty that originally gave him his life. The caterpillar crawls with the dignity of a serpent, eats with the voraciousness of a scavenger, repels potential predators by his repulsive appearance, and eventually succumbs and enters his tomb to be transfigured and redeemed.

The caterpillar who ate as he was supposed to eat, fended for his physical survival consistent with his best instincts, and blessed with the Divine probability of the "chosen," will maintain life. He will eventually wrap himself in the embalmer's bandages of his own spittle to come forth as a celestial creature radiant and esteemed for its beauty, now endowed with the creative ability to recreate himself as he had originally been created.

Interpretations: Spiritual Knowledge

Thanks to the confusion created by many religious teachers who have chosen to confuse rather than enlighten, there is in modern society a poor understanding of spiritual knowledge. Most people consider spiritual knowledge to be so abstract and complicated that only a few can understand it and even fewer can interpret it. This has created an unhealthy dependence on the self-proclaimed interpreters and a very low self-esteem among those who have come seeking understanding. Though there are certainly levels of complexity that only the experienced and the initiated can fully understand, there are essentials which all human beings cannot only fully grasp, but must fully grasp in order to be all that they can be. As we noted above, the most simple of these ideas are built into the very patterns and images of the natural world, which do not lie hidden but are available for the consumption of all who will simply apply their senses.

This story of the butterfly has been used in many different religious traditions and can be understood at multiple levels and in a variety of ways. In fact, one of the characteristics of spiritual knowledge is that it does not follow a one-to-one interpretation. Physical and material knowledge follow the one-to-one correspondence of what appears causative and alike. Material knowledge would suggest to us that a worm is a worm and a butterfly is a butterfly, because their observable characteristics are so different. It would be illogical to argue that the same creature that we see crawling about the leaves in its distasteful form is the same creature that soars in the sky with its beautiful wings and graceful form. This is the conclusion of the materially logical mind: identity is defined by its observable qualities and all identities are distinct and different based upon those particular critical qualities. Death is the cessation of life, so it is materially inconceivable that a thing can be both alive and dead.

Spiritual knowledge is not locked into such "logical precision." Similarity is enough to imply on the (spiritual plane) sameness of identity. *Potential* physical manifestation is actual identification of a thing. What it can or will become is what it is already. Spiritual reality is not subject to the illusions of physical perception. The appearances of the observable can often deceive us about the true and real quality of a thing. The spiritual and religious teachers have always tried to instruct us into the dangers of accepting the *illusions* as the *real*. Spiritual knowledge has always given greater substance to the unperceived than to the perceived. In fact, the spiritual significance of this butterfly story is in its unseen processes and its illogical continuity rather than in the most precise observance of its appearance. Most spiritual systems of interpretation (called religions) have always addressed some of the invisible concepts revealed in the life cycle of this butterfly. For example, the idea of transformation has been explained in the religious terminology of **resurrection, salvation,** or **transcendence.** What was explained in (often very complex) metaphorical pictures was the process of the continuity of life as is so graphically revealed in the life cycle of the butterfly. Since the continuing substance of life is so unavailable for inspection in the human life form, it has been coded in the picture language of the enlightened spiritual teachers. The concept of ghosts, spirits, the **Ba** (from ancient Egypt) as the winged soul of man, are all metaphorical religious

Natural Psychology and Human Transformation

images of this spiritual process of human transformation.

The major and clearest spiritual message of this butterfly story when we apply it to human beings is that *the material manifestations of life are an illusion.* The spot of liquid that looked like a formless nothing was in its essence a very real something. The offensive appearance of the caterpillar was again a stage in a higher and more beautiful life form. The easily committed error with either of these images would have been to conclude that the observable form at any given point was all that there was to be. This does not mean that material reality is not real. It is very much real, as the sustaining and necessary work of the egg and the caterpillar were real. Without either of them there would be no butterfly. Clearly, the survival strategies of the caterpillar were critical to the future birth and expression of its higher life. The leaves that were eaten had to be eaten. The caterpillar would have aborted its own development if it had taken a perpetual fast in anticipation of its future life development. The spiritual message is that the parts do not constitute the whole of life. Life is a whole process and it must be understood as a part of the whole and must be interpreted within the light of its whole expression. Therefore, as human beings, we must engage in the work of the physical world. Eating, sleeping, maneuvering in the physical universe, expressing our physical appetites is not contradictory to our spiritual existence. Many religious teachers have argued that the need to see those physical appetites in the higher and whole sense requires us to negate them as unreal and unnecessary. We should see them as simply requiring restraint because they lead us to a higher reality. We should not automatically negate them as **mere** physical expressions. The butterfly's story gives us a balanced understanding that the "worm" in our nature is not to be condemned as negative nor is it to be indulged as the end of all life. Material needs and wants are necessary appetites which move us towards acquiring future higher goals. The caterpillar needed to consume as many of the leaves as he possibly could. The more he ate and the better that he ate, the more effective would be his future metamorphosis.

This illustration of the illusionary or unreal quality of partial pictures of life is also a message of hope and faith. Very often our appearance is not very appealing in the material assessments of those who perceive us "in part" rather than "in whole." We often suffer great despair because we are judged on the basis of our worm-like appearances. The "nerd" in the school classroom is often repulsive to his more popular and attractive classmates. The proverbial story of the "ugly duckling" who becomes the beautiful swan is the essence of this idea. This same nerd may become the future designer, director, attorney or even plastic surgeon who actually defines or constructs the later standards of beauty. Human beings need to be aware of their whole life process. They need to be taught to see themselves in the fullness of their development so that they are not deceived by the illusions of physical appearance.

In cultures where spiritual knowledge is strong and people learn early that the *invisible* is more real than the *visible*, there is much greater hope and stronger faith. African-American people should have despaired from the 400 years of devastating physical conditions which were experienced during slavery and its aftermath. They should have given up early in the slavery process and relinquished their struggles toward survival. They were locked into perpetual struggle just to maintain life, and their appearance was culturally defined as offensive and hopelessly distasteful. The African appearance was defined as repulsive as that of the hairy worm. However, the African-American people have persisted. They had great faith and were not demoralized even by the painful conditions of their suffering. Because of the strong spiritual consciousness which they had retained from their African cultural experience, they were able to endure when by all logical considerations there was little hope. People despair and relinquish their hold on human decency and dignity when they lose the "whole" picture of life. The caterpillar who fails to realize instinctively its future potential and whole (holy) nature is destined to despair. The decline of spiritual consciousness among African-American people in recent generations has made us much more vulnerable to the despair which comes from appearances. People in less spiritual cultures, who commit suicide when there is a transitory set-back in their financial or material status, have completely lost touch with the wholeness of their being. African-Americans, who in previous generations were almost completely invulnerable to such despair, have in recent times become the most likely to give up life and dignity when appearances seem difficult.

The other interpretative message which emerges from the butterfly image is the importance of perseverance. Certainly, the natural consequence of faith is persistence. The ability to stick with a struggle when all appearances suggest that the victory cannot be attained is a consequence of seeing the **whole** picture. Spiritual knowledge helps us to gain a full picture of the whole and we are therefore better equipped to persevere when things look rough or even impossible. A worm who only sees itself as a worm is not as likely to continue in the struggles of consuming the leaves. A worm who understands that it is in the process of becoming a butterfly and realizes that its struggles are only a means to a bigger end, will persist. This is no doubt the kind of knowledge that inspired our noble ancestors such as Harriet Tubman, Sojourner Truth, Elijah Muhammad and so many other notables from our American history experience. But it must have been this larger picture which also inspired our grandmothers, grandfathers, and parents to persist against overwhelming odds. The ability to see the "big picture" is crucial in mastering the challenges to life.

The many and varied religious traditions which African-American people have historically followed (and continue to follow), have all been varying "languages" to identify this bigger picture. When the language of those religions provide the inspiration to see the bigger picture, those religions are valid and useful. However, when one leaves the church, mosque, temple or hall and only has images of material shortcomings, that religion has become dysfunctional. When the religion only creates a transcendent vision which fails to inspire the people to attend to their material and contemporary condition and to engage in steps of self-improvement, the religion is dysfunctional. Remember, the caterpillar does not cease to eat because it is destined to become a butterfly; in fact, it eats that much more voraciously because of some instinctive knowledge of its destiny. So it must be the same for us. We must labor persistently because of our awareness of our spiritual destiny. The caterpillar's "vision" is built into its instinct and we must build our vision from solid knowledge of truth and our destiny.

Interpretations: Transformation

Probably the most important idea which comes from the butterfly story is the idea that life evolves or unfolds through a series of births and deaths. This evolution or unfoldment is referred to as transformation. The movement through a variety of forms is how the human life is ultimately manifested in its true or spiritual form.

The first life form is essentially characterized as gross matter or a physical form. The qualities that characterize the functioning of the "physical" are qualities which are associated with the material or the enhancement of the material manifestation. As we saw in the characteristics of the caterpillar, which is the initial manifestation of the butterfly life form, the first form is one that is primarily physical in its orientation. (The egg is actually only potential life in an undifferentiated form). As the caterpillar is focused on the building up of the physical form, the initial human requirement as an individual and as a society is to build ourselves as physical life forms.

Individually, feeding on food and basic knowledge as well as the gradual acquisition of height and bulk are the earliest manifestations of growth. Life is sustained once a basic physical presence has been established. The primary provision of parents is to provide for the physical well-being of the new offspring. Human beings need to establish themselves with food, shelter and clothing in order to establish a foundation for their continued growth.

Societies or communities must begin to grow in the same way. The society or community must initially focus on the basics for survival. They must control some land and the resources for life which emerge from the land. There must be the establishment of influence over how you will eat and how you will preserve yourself as a physical entity. This is the foundation for your economic system. Economics has its importance, not in the superior value of the material, but in the necessity of the material for the maintenance of the physical life. As a consequence, all of the other components of a society must grow from this foundation. As the caterpillar demonstrates, if you do not eat adequately in this initial stage, your future development will be clearly jeopardized.

There should be no argument about the necessity of material things. The difficulty arises with the perverse preoccupation with the material. "Materialism" is the establishment of materials as the ultimate objective and value of the person and the society. Materials are a *means* to an *end* and not an end in itself. The economic resources which sustain us materially are not the totality of our being. The difficulty faced in the modern Western world is the preoccupation with economics as the primary agenda for all of life. It is this preoccupation that has reduced us to a caterpillar people, consumed by consumption. The human nature, as is the nature of the caterpillar, is to rise to a higher life from--to be transformed. Under normal conditions (and of course, assuming survival), the caterpillar naturally transforms. With the human being, there must be an environment that keeps the consciousness of his higher potential within his thinking. If the environment does not give him a vision of his higher human possibilities, then he will perceive himself as no more than a caterpillar and will die as a worm.

The worst of circumstances is a society that not only fails to bring consciousness of the higher human potential, but actually encourages the caterpillar to remain a worm. A society that rewards and values physical and material goals and encourages people to see themselves only as physical entities, is a society which abnormally stifles genuine human transformation. The consequence is to create a society filled with overgrown worms. In scriptural and symbolic language, the worm is often a symbol for the degraded human being who is nasty, unattractive and undeveloped in its civilized form. These worm-like creatures are preoccupied with expanding themselves physically. They eat when they are not hungry and acquire wealth only to hoard wealth. They are terrified of death and are actually horrified by any indications of decline in their physical youthfulness. These worms have grown comfortable with their caterpillar stage. They can destroy themselves by stifling their ultimate human form. It is vital that human beings develop a higher spiritual vision. If they do not, they will be born as worms and will die as worms, to ultimately become food for the worms.

Proper human transformation requires that human beings take responsibility for their effective unfolding. They must recognize their physical necessities and attend to their provision.

They must make the kinds of selections from the "leaves" of the environment to insure that they "eat to live." As we have suggested in our description of the caterpillar, he must eat selectively to insure his future evolution. Since human beings are not guided by instinct in this regard, we must bring knowledge to our selections to insure that our consumption is consistent with our best self-interest. The large number of preventable deaths in Western society, despite great abundance, is indicative of the consequence of careless consumption. Not only do we eat too many of the wrong kinds of foods, we also consume toxins with an assured negative effect on our bodies. Our failure to select the kinds of "leaves" that will insure our survival is the basis of the major reasons for our failure to survive even in the physical form. If one doesn't survive in the fundamental stages of his physical development, then transformation becomes an impossibility. Life can deteriorate and become deformed. This deformity simply returns life to an even more basic form such as back to the minerals of its pre-embryonic existence.

In very similar fashion, the society that fails to lay the proper physical foundation handicaps its future transformation or destroys itself, as does the individual who eats improperly. As we have discussed above, the society must be rooted on a firm physical or economic basis in order to continue to grow. If the society does not develop a means of production for the basic necessities of its people, that society is essentially doomed. As historically oppressed or colonized people move towards some degree of independence in a society, they must develop a sense of industry and formulate some concept for developing themselves materially. If they do not, they are certainly handicapping themselves by a persisting dependency which will insure their continued captivity. This painful picture certainly is true in the lives of African-American people who, despite 100 years off of the plantations and with considerable development within the confines of the European-American society remain handicapped and dependent on the goodwill of our former captors for all of the necessities of survival. We have considerable resources but there is no method of autonomous direction for those resources because we have failed to develop a sense of industry which would require us to control some of the basic processes for our survival as a people. We can gain a greater appreciation for other formerly captive people who have insisted at the price of death that they must maintain a homeland, even if the majority of their people do not reside there. The transformation into a society does not occur if people do not initially establish a foundation to control the processes of production for themselves.

Interpretation: Forming the Cocoon (Society)

As we observed in the description of the caterpillar above, after feeding for a period of time, the worm begins to emit out of his mouth a silky substance. He then begins to roll himself into this silk-like shroud or covering. The implication from this natural picture is that once the physical life has been established, you must prepare yourself for greater growth. In order to achieve a higher and a new form of growth, it is necessary to create a new kind of environment. This new environment must surround your life-form in such a way that you are permitted to continue the process of transformation. If we can digress briefly to the physical development of the human being, we observe that the prenatal environment is very different from the postnatal one. The qualities of the prenatal environment are absolutely conducive for the very best growth of the human embryo. The environment of the womb provides the proper kind of nourishment, security and conditions for the growth of the fertilized human egg to become an infant. At the conclusion of about nine months of growth, the human infant must change its environment in order to continue to grow. Though the environment of the mother's womb was highly adequate for a preliminary growth in order for the human being's growth to continue, it will be necessary for it to have another kind of environment. This is also the case for the caterpillar's continued development. It is very instructive about the importance of proper environmental conditions for the establishment of proper growth and development.

So, while the tree environment was perfect for the growth of the caterpillar, a new environment must be created in order for real transformation to occur. This is what the cocoon is about. It represents the establishment of a proper environment to facilitate continued growth. For the process of human transformation, we can refer to this cocoon as a **society.** The society is the "covering" of culture which ensures that life will continue to unfold as it should. In the tree environment, guided by appetite and physical needs, a worm can only remain a worm. The tree "womb" is more than adequate for the earliest development of the caterpillar life, but if the caterpillar is ever to become something greater, it must alter its environment. In much the same way, human beings must be contained in an environment that permits them to advance to a higher plane. There are several lessons to be learned about the nature of the cocoon which the human being needs in order to advance the unfoldment of their higher human potential.

On the one hand, the growth process is an individual phenomenon. However, the growth must occur within the confines of a group, i.e., the society. We depend upon others to help us construct our cocoon. The nature of the cocoon which is needed for human growth requires the input and cooperation of other human beings. Transformation will not occur by withdrawing from the critical elements of society. We require guidance which has been placed in the repository of the traditional wisdom of the culture and society. The keys to proper human growth have been planted in the fabric of the culture. We must grow into the society and into the life of the proper culture in order to obtain access to these keys. Though it is possible to choose a transient reclusive life, the translation of nature's (The Neter's) lessons must be obtained through the keys which reside in the cultural life of the society. Withdrawing from the society does not build a person. A society builds a person. In order for proper human growth to occur, however, the cocoon must be a proper cocoon established out of one's own spittle (or nature). Life will not grow in an alien cocoon. The compelling picture of the caterpillar is how it spits from its **own** mouth the cocoon which must contain it. The culture is the silk-like substance which must enclose the human form in order for it to be properly transformed. The culture must be an authentic one that represents the true nature of the human being that it is to help grow. There are several kinds of insects that establish cocoons for growth, but the caterpillar must establish its own cocoon based upon the substance of its mouth. As mentioned above, the society must have been firmly established on a material basis to insure the kind of independence and autonomy which will let it establish its indigenous culture.

The caterpillar had to consume special kinds of leaves. The leaves had to be of the proper character to assure that its future developmental environment would be of the highest quality. He had to eat leaves with the proper moisture to assure that the consistency of the cocoon would be strong enough to secure him for continued growth. In much the same way, human culture must have the proper amount of moisture in it to assure that the growth will be adequate. We can think of water content as the spiritual or moral component of the society. Morality is the rigor that maintains spiritual direction. Moral strength is the quality which cultivates proper choices and proper orientation. These are the principles which guide life in its proper and natural direction. Contrary to the distortions created by many religious cults, morality is not a cage which confines the human passions. The human passions are natural when properly guided. Morality provides the proper guidance which channels those passions towards the objective of higher human unfoldment. The society becomes the enforcer and reinforcer of the proper orientations which insure this natural and higher evolution. Human beings are all equipped with a *will* which is the divine enforcer which we have within us. The will brings regulation to the passions which transforms them into higher expressions that drive the life to a higher manifestation.

Morality permits the establishment of self-rule. In order to achieve the higher human destiny of rulership in the earth, humans must establish rulership within themselves. The temptation to remain in the condition of self-indulgence, which characterized the caterpillar's form, often serves as a barrier to achieving the higher growth. The power which overcomes the gravity of the lower appetites is the force of the will, which pulls the person to a higher growth. The society must cultivate this quality in order to feed the higher growth. A primitive society or culture is one that fosters the lower appetites and encourages the posture of the worm. Such a society is one that will fail in providing the kind of environment which facilitates higher growth. Such a society keeps people in the worm state by constantly encouraging self-indulgence, material appetites and obscuring the ultimate evolutionary form of human beings.

The society is built from the mouth of the worm. From the mouth come the **words** which are the knowledge base of the culture. In addition to the morality, the next cultural ingredient for the society must be knowledge. This knowledge represents the direction to the path of Truth. All of the learning acquired by people must provide guidance to the ultimate path of Truth. Truth is the substantive form of nature in her proper order and form. Science, philosophy, math, art, music, history, geography, etc., are all descriptions of how the Neters express themselves. Though societies are constantly evolving in their ability to describe these manifestations of Truth, the knowledge base of the society constitutes the best and most honest description of nature in her proper order. This knowledge transmitted by the society to the person becomes the foundation for guidance and the evolution of the mind, as the person learns to read the Divine messages found in nature's proper order. Even a people's understanding of their unique and special history is a description of the human progress and form offered from the perspective of one's particular people experience. The knowledge base must be appropriate to the people being taught because the special message in a people's culture is a special set of keys for each culture to grow itself consistent with its own nature and its own way.

Each word of knowledge becomes a strand of silk emerging from the mouths of the teachers and the Elders. This knowledge offers insight into the processes of growth, transformation and Divine order, consequently feeding the ultimate evolution of life to its highest form. The teachers of truth continue to spew forth the words of proper growth despite opposition and the illusions of greater power being contained elsewhere. They understand that the message of their lessons is to help the society to transform the people.

A societal culture with a proper material or economic base and a moral balance that is rooted in a firm knowledge oriented towards Truth will naturally begin to generate a new form of life. As people begin to think differently and see themselves differently, a new kind of human development begins to occur. People are no longer satisfied with limited and material goals. People no longer seek to satisfy most base "worm" desires. Instead, people begin to forge new definitions, concepts, relationships, and ultimately new societal structures which perpetuate the new kind of growth. Gradually, the old songs, dances and artwork begin to disappear. Societal customs regarding relationships begin to change in accord with the new definitions of people. The entire culture is raised up to a higher plane in accord with the higher form of knowledge which is feeding the minds of the people.

The politics or organizational structure does not follow the guidelines of the old societal form. The distribution and utilization of power and influence within the society must also be consistent with the leaves of knowledge which are growing the new society. Imitation and modification of the older forms will be inadequate since these forms were grown out of another knowledge base. In other words, this new cocoon must be altered rather thoroughly in order to develop a new life form. This is a tremendous challenge, but we can see that the world's oldest peoples have labored for thousands of years to create the kinds of traditions and knowledge which would create another concept of human being. Modernism or modernity has become a new code word for the imposition of the cultural characteristics of European-American, Judeo-Christian values on the entirety of humanity. The consequence has been the construction of a worldwide set of clones of the Euro-American cultural form. By people sacrificing their indigenous cultural forms, they have also sacrificed their mechanism for effective human growth and transformation.

Why do human beings need their own society and culture? As the butterfly shows us, we cannot grow and be transformed without a natural and proper society within which to develop ourselves. Individual efforts of transformation only work minimally and are ultimately doomed to failure because of the absence of the transformational shroud offered by the "society." The old life must die in order for the new life to be born. Death never comes without a resistance. Until we place ourselves within the confines of a womb or environment that feeds our natural growth, that provides moral guidance and nourishes us with knowledge of Truth, we cannot grow to a higher form. We must have an educational system that gives our children correct and proper information about themselves and their ultimate human potential. If they are taught that their greatest assets are their physical characteristics, they will emphasize those physical characteristics as their agenda. If they value sports and play in preference to intellect and ideas, we will continue to produce "gang-bangers" and football players, rather than scholars and builders.

We are taught that the ancient Africans built for eternity. They saw the human life as an eternal process. They did not see their physical lifetime as the duration of their possibility. They understood that every life born had a responsibility of helping to construct the cocoon which would serve as an environment of growth for generations yet unborn. The monuments, symbols and rituals which were developed were intended to offer people a much larger vision of their lives. When you have stopped attending to the fleeting images of a transitory world and are fed by eternal images of permanence, continuity and timelessness, you begin to lay the foundation for building pyramids and Temples of learning, rather than skyscrapers and teaching laboratories. You begin to see the universe as your home as opposed to a small mansion on a hill in Beverly Hills as your dwelling place.

Interpretation: The Birth of the Butterfly

In this proper societal cocoon, the worm begins to fade away. Nothing supernatural happens. No entity comes down from the clouds, nor does a psychedelic explosion take place in the brain. As you enclose yourself in a natural and Truth-based cocoon, the old form begins to fall away and a new form begins to come into being. The worm's form begins to disintegrate within the confines of the silken cocoon. The simple cylinder shape of a worm gives way to the more complex structure which begins to manifest itself with sprouting wings. Within the confines of the cocoon, the multiple legs made for crawling begin to melt away. Soon, the despicable appearance of the hairy worm begins to disappear and a new life that went into the cocoon crawling is ready to emerge capable of flight. It went in looking gray and crude and it comes out in multiple colors which blend with the sun and the flowers and even the colors of the rainbow. It went into the cocoon only capable of eating leaves, but it emerges capable of eating from the higher regions of the upper world. It went in being underfoot and vulnerable to all of the earthly creatures, but it emerges capable of sailing above the heads of most of its former foes. It went in moving slowly, restricted to the world of one tree, but it comes out flying over many trees and vulnerable only to other celestial creatures.

Societies and cultures provide the same transformative shield for its people. It is within the society that crude and worm-like people enter as crawling and vulnerable creatures. Their condition is appalling and their progress is slow to the observing eye. When the society invests the people with a vision, they are able to persist in their toil while not becoming distracted by their work. They understand that their material journey is a temporary one and they do not see their current objectives as being their ultimate objectives. Like the caterpillar, they trudge along eating the leaves of the material tree, understanding that their labors are ultimately for a higher life. They neither despise nor glorify their labors as being their destiny. When the developing human being commits himself to a constructive cocoon (culture/society), he realizes that the elegance of individuality is lost in the higher glamour of the cocoon that ultimately transforms. There is no strong commitment to the worm-like form. Though they value, protect and nurture their caterpillar status, they do not invest the full energies of their lives into the separate and incompletely developed form. Within the cocoon, one gives up the illusion of ego or separateness and takes on the transformative power of the society. There is a sacrifice of some of one's smaller form, but it only serves to manifest the higher, larger and more perfect human form.

The society, through its education and institutions, and the culture with its symbols, rituals and concepts, must constantly keep the vision of a higher and more perfect human form alive. People must see themselves as servants to the higher Truth which has shaped them and determined their destiny. They must also see themselves as servants to each other and the vessels for the manifestation for the highest virtues of life-such as creativity, truth, harmony, righteousness, thought and love. A society which transmits these concepts to its inhabitants and cultivates this consciousness into its people, is a society which has the transformative power of the butterfly's cocoon. Such people understand the importance of loyalty, self-knowledge, self-mastery and self-preservation. Such people understand the power of love, kindness, benevolence, sensitivity, sacrifice and perseverance because these are the qualities of the higher human form (colors of the butterfly). They learn to obey the laws of civility and nature, not out of fear of damnation and intimidation by a punitive and vindictive higher power, but out of fear of the loss of connection with the highest principles of the universe into which they are intricately tied.

To emerge from the cocoon as a butterfly person means that horizons will be opened everywhere which are as limitless as the sky. (It's probably for this reason that the ancient Masters taught that "heaven" was in the sky). Unlike the caterpillar, butterflies are masters of the earth, of gravity and of the powers of the physical form. What they cannot control, they can at least regulate or transcend. When it is necessary to eat from the earth, like the butterfly, they can swoop down to the earth and drink of the nectar of the sweetest flowers. Your very form and rhythm invites admiration from other creatures. The flight of the transformed butterfly person will not be heavy, because she has mastered the gravity of the earth, its materials and the control of the physical form which is the source of weight. Such people have become so light, that like a butterfly (though more massive than the caterpillar predecessor), they can sit on a rose petal and drink from the nectar of its heart and the life of the flower is undisturbed. Such "lightness" is indicative of having found harmony with the natural creation.

This process of human transformation is as natural and real for the human being as it is for the butterfly. Ancient people of Africa and Asia have long identified human transformation as a natural and necessary process. Those societies have always emphasized spiritual goals for their people and spiritual objectives for their institutions. This does not mean that such societies ignore technological and economic goals of feeding the caterpillar nature of the people, but the higher goals have been the ones of building civility towards others, respect for those who have mastered and managed the process of transformation, and developing a consciousness of **The God** in the minds of the people. Such societies served to foster this process of transformation and obtained peace and prosperity for many centuries as a result. All of these societies have deviated from the higher course from time-to-time and have been pulled or arrested into a caterpillar state. Such societies actually retard the process of human transformation rather than facilitating it as their purpose.

Conclusion

From the earliest records of human history, there is a clear indication of the human aspiration for a higher life. In the most wondrous of ancient societies, such as the Kemites (called Egyptians) and the Mayans, it was clear that this vision of a higher spiritual possibility predominated the concerns of these great people. We still puzzle over the construction of the ancient Kemetic monuments, temples and "mysteries" as we puzzle over the former greatness and accomplishments of the Mayans and so many other great people of the Earth's southern hemisphere. We find evidence that these societies were superbly capable of mastering technology and, in fact, had superior technical knowledge to the modern world (witness the still not replicated construction of the Great Pyramid of Giza). These people managed to feed themselves, develop methods of transportation and communication, and deal with the social and physical realities of a material world. Despite attending to their material existence, they did not falter in their vision of a higher reality and a higher human potential. Most of their societal energies were obviously devoted to worship of **The God**, and education of the society into a higher and transformative consciousness.

The story of the transformation of the butterfly is a very simple but revealing image of the illusions of our material eyes. It is certainly conceivable that if a caterpillar can only be a fleeting illusion of a higher butterfly life, why shouldn't our material form and preoccupations be a fleeting illusion of our greater butterfly-like capabilities. Every society has been gifted with prophets, seers and teachers who have helped to focus our vision on our greater human capability or to offer their example of what the transformed human being looks like. However, our records of truly transformed people emerging from a transformative

The Society and the Butterfly

society are not clear at all. Many religious communities claim such feats, but the evidence of their categorical success is suspect. In fact, their more recent versions are in the forms of cults like the ones which were incinerated in a Texas town or committed mass suicide in a Guyana jungle. These are only perverse forms which have preyed on the vision still latent in the consciousness of people to be transformed into butterflies by a society with a vision.

We have discussed the characteristics of the caterpillar, the cocoon and the butterfly. We are less clear on how to construct the right and proper cocoon which will transform worms to butterflies. There are several things that we already know for sure. So-called modern Western society has arrested human development, creating and perpetuating a massive caterpillar plague, and has served to clearly endanger the life of the butterfly in the modern world. Its emphasis on materialism, the feeding and stimulating of the lower human appetites, and the rational discreditation of spiritual reality are all elements which have eroded the modern cocoon's ability to transform human beings. The consequence is the epidemic of human problems of the most savage forms such as child molestation, cannibalism, family dissolution, eroded human relationships and self-destructive conduct of all forms.

We have also tried to describe what the cocoon should look like. We talked about its qualities and its responsibilities. When great visionaries such as Muhammad and Jesus (may peace be upon both of them) challenged their societies, they either had to engage in warfare or meet their death at the hands of the opposition. This suggests that though the transformative cocoon is a natural state and it ultimately serves the purpose of humanity's higher destiny, to spin this cocoon is no simple task. Such efforts will inevitably be met by opposition from forces which would profit and be empowered by humanity's arrested development.

Right-minded people who hold the vision and have some consciousness of their higher human capability must come together in order to wrestle control of the forces of the society. Those who have been the greatest victims of misused societal powers and misguided "worms" who seek to block the emergence of butterflies must draw upon their historical experiences to discredit the false promises of an oppressive reality. People who have been historically oppressed by materialism, racism and sexism must join forces against these processes in the society and must help to forge a truly transformative society free of these forces.

We must trust and build on the vision that human beings are capable and destined to be butterflies. We cannot give credence and preeminence to images which are determined to reduce the human potential to murder, warfare, greed and debauchery. We must lift up and exemplify in our own conduct, the very best potential of human beings. We must care for each other in an active form of service so that the benevolent force of the higher Truth can be reflected through us. We must become servants of humanity and servants of the Higher Vision. We must lend our talents (whatever they may be) to the liberation and elevation of the human spirit by **"whatever means necessary."**

References

Guthrie, Robert. *Even the Rat was White*. San Diego: Dunbar Press, 1976.

Thomas, A. & Sillen, S. *Racism and Psychiatry*. New York: Bruner/Mazel Pub., 1972.

Also by Na'im Akbar...

Books:

Chains and Images of Psychological Slavery

The Community of Self

From Miseducation to Education

Visions for Black Men

Light from Ancient Africa

Audio and video cassettes of Na'im Akbar's lectures are also available from:

Mind Productions & Associates, Inc.
P. O. Box 11221
Tallahassee, FL 32302
(904) 222-1764